THE
JOKE BOOK

Other joke books available in Armada

Christmas Crackers 1 and 2
2nd Armada Book of Jokes and Riddles
Crazy - But True!
Crazy Curriculum
Compiled by Jonathan Clements

The Awful Joke Book
The Most Awful Joke Book Ever
The Batty Book Book
The Batty Cartoon Book
How Trivial Can You Get?
Edited by Mary Danby

The Schoolkids' Joke Book
Compiled by Brough Girling

Holiday Joke Book
Bill Howard

The Grisley Joke Book
Compiled by David Pugh

Ghostly Gags
Alan Robertson

THE TEDDY BEAR JOKE BOOK

GYLES BRANDRETH
Illustrated by Alan Snow

An Armada Original

First published in the U.K. in 1990 in Armada

Armada is an imprint of the Children's Division,
part of the Harper Collins Publishing Group,
8 Grafton Street, London W1X 3LA.

Text © Complete Editions 1990
Illustrations © Alan Snow 1990

Printed and bound in Great Britain by
William Collins Sons & Co. Ltd., Glasgow

To my bear
GROWLER

Knock Knock!
Who's there?
Fozzie!
Fozzie Who?
Fozzie hundredth time, turn over ze
page,
I want to read ze book!

Introduction

Welcome to the cuddly world of teddy bears!

I hope that all of you have a special bear at home that you love to hug when you're feeling happy ... or maybe your teddy cheers you up when you're feeling sad and lonely ... or perhaps he lets you hide behind him when you're watching something scary on the telly ... ?

Whatever your bear does, you love him.

Everybody loves teddy bears, and that's what makes them special ... from the very first teddy in 1902 (named after the then President of the United States of America — Teddy Roosevelt) to the present day teddy stars like Sooty and Superted ... to your own rather old teddy bear, who might have a patch over one eye and might be losing a bit of stuffing . . . all bears are loveable.

This book of jokes is a small tribute to the teddy bear . . . it follows the teddy bear around the world, into the kitchen, onto the sports field and back into your home . . . I hope that you giggle a little as you read through these pages with your bear sitting on your lap.

I hope that your teddy bear giggles a little too!

OK teddies, grab your hats and honey pots . . . we're off!

Bears Everywhere!

Why do you sleep so well when
you're cuddling a teddy bear?
Teddy bears don't snore!

What's brown, furry and red?
A blushing teddy bear!

What do you call a teddy bear
wearing five balaclavas?
Anything you want, he won't hear
you!

What does a bear need if he's going
to be a record-breaker?
Ted-ication!

What do you get if you cross a teddy
with a brass musical instrument?
A Tu-bear!

What do teddy bears do when they
have toothache?
They just grin and bear it!

Where does a bear buy his phone?
From British Teddy-com!

What's the difference between a teddy bear and an apple?
Teddy bears don't grow on trees.

10

Customer: "I say, I say, I say, do you sell teddy bear's food?"
Shop-owner: "Only if they bring money with them!"

Why didn't the millionaire teddy bear ever have a bath? Because he was filthy rich!

What is the most successful teddy
bear pop group ever?
Bear-nanarama!

Why did the teddy bear cross the
road?
To show that he wasn't chicken!

Who brings teddy bears all
their Christmas presents?
Santa-Paws!

What does a teddy bear become
after it's six months old?
Seven months old!

What newspaper does a bear read?
The Daily Teddy-graph!

Who's it's Boss?
The Ted-itor!

Why did the teddy bear take a day off
school?
He was feeling rather paw-ly!

13

Jack: Dad, Jill's broken my teddy bear!
Dad: How did she do that?
Jack: I hit her over the head with it!

What do teddy bears do when it rains?
They get wet!

Where's the safest place to be when your teddy bear's in a bad mood!
As fur away as possible!

Jack: What's your favourite star?
Jill: The Great Bear!

What's brown, furry, is very good at adding up, and lives in Australia?
A Koala bear with a calculator.

Why do polar bears find it so hard to keep secrets?
Because they are always chattering in the Arctic!

What's a polar bear's favourite
breakfast?
Ice crispies.

Why did teddy take off his shoes?
He wanted to bear his soles!

How do bears watch EastEnders?
On a teddy-vision!

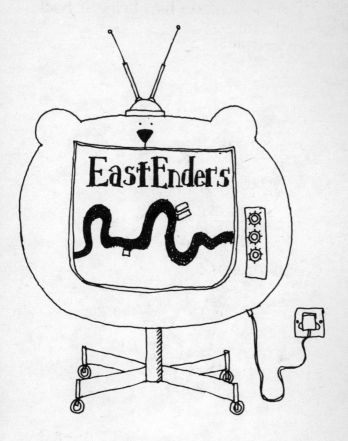

Why do grizzly bears have long fur?
Because there aren't any barbers in
the forest.

What happened to the teddy bear
that ran away with the circus?
The Police made him bring it back
again!

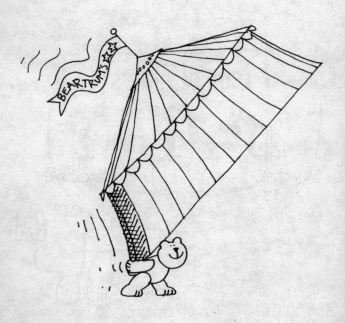

Why are polar bears white?
There are no sunny beaches in the
Arctic!

Why, if there are no sunny beaches in the Arctic, do polar bears wear sunglasses?
They like pretending to be pandas!

Why are there so many dents in a polar bear's front door?
Because he keeps bumping into it.
Why?
He can't see properly when he's wearing his panda disguise!

What happened when the panda
realised that his best friend was really
a polar bear in disguise?
There was absolute panda-monium!

What do you call a teddy bear
who's lost his fur?
Fred-bear!

Jack: I've just got a teddy bear for my sister!
Jamie: That sounds like a good deal!

Why did the teddy hide behind the sofa during the horror movie?
He couldn't bear the suspense!

Pooh, why have you got your head in a honey pot?

I'm sorry, I can't hear you! My head's stuck in this honey pot!

One fine day, a teddy bear walked into a coffee bar and ordered a glass of milk.

The man behind the counter was astonished to meet a talking teddy bear but he served him all the same. The bear drank his milk quietly, without slurping, and then gave the man a five pound note. The man, who wasn't very nice, didn't think a teddy bear could possibly understand money, so he tricked him by only giving him one pound change:

"I hope you enjoyed your glass of milk," he said to the bear, "We don't get many teddy bears coming in here, you know!"

"With prices like yours," replied the bear, "I'm not surprised!"

Which teddy bears have their eyes nearest together?
The smallest teddy bears!

What can't a teddy bear
ever make right?
His left paw!

What shampoo does a bear always
use?
Ted-and-Shoulders!

Why are teddy bears always so
happy?
Because they're made in stitches!

How do you make a teddy bear?
Take off his clothes!

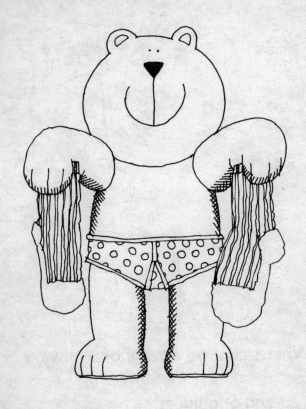

What do all good bears put in their
cars' petrol tanks?
Un-Tedded petrol!

What does a teddy bear put in his house?
Fur-niture!

How do teddy bears keep their houses cool in the hot summer?
They use bear-conditioning!

Why did Jamie dress his teddy bear in a red, white and blue outfit?
Because the teddy bear couldn't dress himself!

Jamie: What kind of bear is that?
Zookeeper: A Police bear!
Jamie: I've never heard of such a thing!
Zookeeper: You've never heard of a Police bear?
Jamie: No, and anyway . . . he doesn't look like a Police bear!
Zookeeper: That's because he's a Plain Clothes Ted-ective!

Tuck in with Teddy!

It is a well known fact that teddy bears love their food.

Winnie-the-Pooh loves honey ... Paddington loves marmalade ... but what does your bear like? The only way to find out is if we go into the kitchen and have a look around at all the lovely things that are kept hidden away in all the dark, exciting cup-boards ...

The only problem is that all the tasty things are usually kept on the shelves that you and I can't reach aren't they?! ... Never mind, it won't be too long before we get chocolate pudding again ... in the meantime, here are some tasty teddy-ticklers from the kitchen!

What do you get if you cross
a teddy bear with a pig?
Furry sausages?

What did the fat teddy bear say when he sat down to eat his supper?
I'm afraid that this is all going to waist!

What's pink and white and flies at 500 mph?
Superted's ham sandwich!

What's the difference between a teddy bear and a turkey?
If you don't know that, then I'm not asking you to cook Christmas dinner!

What's a bear's favourite dessert?
Ted-and-butter pudding!

How did Paddington stop his marmalade sandwich going stale?
He ate it!

What do you get if a teddy bear falls
into the gravy?
Soup-a-Ted!

What do you get if you cross a
teddy bear with a mint?
A Polo-bear!

29

Why do teddy bears have black, shiny noses?
So they can hide in the liquorice jar!

What do teddy bears have for breakfast?
Tedded Wheat!

How do you know when a teddy bear's been in the fridge?
By the paw-prints in the butter!

What kind of pasta do all teddy bears love?
Taglia-Teddy!

What do you get when your teddy bear has finished his breakfast?
Breakfast-in-Ted!

What do polar bears
have for lunch?
Ice-Burgers!

Why don't teddy bears eat meat?
Because they're never given any!

What do you do with a green teddy
bear?
Wait till he's ripe!

What do polar bears
call their money?
Iced-lolly!

How does a teddy bear keep his milk
fresh?
He stores it in a bear-tight container!

Shaggy Bear Story

Once upon a time there was a huge grizzly bear who wanted to find out why, of all the bears in the world, he was the biggest and the strongest. After a year or two of wandering and thinking, he came across a polar bear sitting on an iceberg having a nap, so he asked the polar bear, but the polar bear really wasn't very interested and carried on sleeping.

Next, after another couple of years of wandering, the huge grizzly bear came across a black bear sitting on a rock having a sleep, but the black bear wasn't very interested either, and just carried on sleeping.

Next, after another two years of wandering, he met a panda sitting under a tree eating bamboo shoots, but the panda ignored the grizzly bear and just carried on eating.

By now the grizzly bear was getting fed up because he'd asked all the other bears why he was the biggest and the strongest, and they wouldn't tell him.

Then one day, he saw a family having a picnic by a river, and there, with them was a tiny little teddy bear, no bigger than a honey pot. The great big grizzly ran over to the little teddy, looked down at him and said:

"Tell me, teddy bear, why aren't you as big and strong as I am?"

The little teddy bear looked up at the enormous grizzly and said:

"Well, I've not been very well lately!"

What did the school-teacher say to the teddy bear that wouldn't tell the truth?
You're a bear-faced liar!

Why can't Ted the builder find his pick axe? Because today's the day the teddy bears have their picks nicked!

What does a very fat teddy bear have that a very thin teddy bear doesn't have?
A bear-belly!

Three explorers were deep in the middle of a huge forest, when they realised that they were lost.

"Help!" they cried, and almost immediately a voice thundered down from the sky:

"Welcome to the enchanted forest! Your wish is my command!"

"Get me out of here!" said the first traveller ... and he disappeared!

"Turn me into an eagle!" said the second, who squawked and then flew away!

The third traveller was so amazed by what he had just seen, that he walked, in a daze, straight into a smelly swamp.

"Pooh!" he said, and was immediately turned into a teddy bear!

Why didn't the Ancient-Britons have teddy bears?
Because they hadn't been invented yet!

Why did the teddy bear become an electrician?
He was looking for a little light relief!

Old Grampa bear was so old that his fur was beginning to fall out; so he went to see the teddy bear doctor to find a cure:

"Doctor, doctor, can you give me something to stop me losing my fur?"

"Certainly," replied the doctor. "Here's a paper bag — it'll be quite safe in that!"

What do you call a teddy lumberjack? Tim-Bear!

What's white, and travels across ice at 100 mph? A polar bear on a motorbike!

What's cuddly,
and goes
putt-putt?
A teddy bear
playing golf!

Little teddy bear: Golly, did you catch that huge fish all by yourself?
Big teddy bear: No, a little worm helped me!

Old Ted: My fur's getting thinner!
Young Ted: Who wants fat fur anyway?

How do teddy bears read weather?
On a bear-ometer!

Jack: I've lost my teddy bear!
Jamie: Why not put an advertisement
in the paper?
Jack: Don't be silly, he can't read!

What is the highest
teddy bear mountain?
Bear-Nevis!

Why did the little teddy bear
join the Boy Scouts brigade?
Because he was a bear-cub!

What was the teddy bear doing on
the television?
Sleeping (there was no room on the
sofa!)

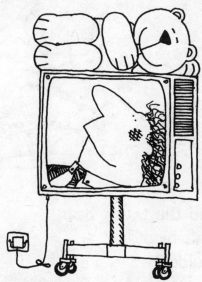

If 97 teddy bears tried to stand under
the same umbrella, why didn't any of
them get wet?
It wasn't raining!

What happens if teddy gets torn?
He runs and runs until he gets a stitch!

What did the teddy bear
get on his birthday?
A year older!

Jamie owned a teddy bear called
Trouble. He called him Trouble because he was always going on long
trips without saying where he was

going. Normally this didn't matter because he usually got back for supper and Jamie's bedtime . . .

But one day Trouble disappeared and didn't come back for supper, and then he didn't come back for bedtime. Jamie lay in bed, and he couldn't get to sleep because he was so worried. At midnight, he decided that he'd better try to find his bear, so he climbed down the drainpipe outside his bedroom window, and ran down the street. Very soon he met a policeman who asked Jamie what he was doing out in the street in the middle of the night dressed only in his pyjamas.

"I'm looking for Trouble!" answered Jamie.

Why are Egyptian teddy bears so well behaved?
Because they respect their Mummies!

Why was the teddy bear wearing dark glasses?
If you had so many jokes made about you, you wouldn't want to be recognised either!

Patient: Doctor, I keep thinking I'm a bear!
Doctor: How long has this been going on?
Patient: Ever since I was a cub!

What's the difference between a
panda and a polar bear?
Oh, about 1500 miles!

Which teddy bear lives
in a greenhouse
in outer-space?
The ozone bear!

What did the old teddy bear say
when he lost all his money on the
horses?
I'm Bruinned!

What do you do if a giant teddy bear stands on your foot?
You wait for him to get off!

What can you see if you're crawling through a tunnel behind a teddy bear?
A Ted-end!

What is furry, cuddly and has ten legs?
Five teddy bears!

Brown teddy bear: Where does that polar bear come from?
Black teddy bear: Alaska.
Brown teddy bear: Don't worry, I'll ask her myself!

Neighbour: Your teddy bear just bit my ankle!
Jill: Well, he's only little, he couldn't reach your knee!

What doesn't growl, but sounds like a bear?
A pear!

Why did the teddy start work in the Doctor's Surgery?
Because he was an Intensive Care-Bear!

When Moses-bear came down from the mountain, what was he carrying?
The Ted Commandments!

What happened to the teddy bear that tried to learn to tap dance?
He fell into the bath!

What's the difference between a
teddy bear and a biscuit?
You don't dunk your teddy bear in
your tea!

What kind of teddy bear can see just
as well out of the back of his head as
the front?
Any teddy bear with his eyes closed!

There once was a teddy called Ted,
Who liked to eat honey in bed.
But one day it spilt
All over his quilt,
So he ate up the pillow instead.

What do you call a polar bear in the jungle?
Lost!

Where was the teddy bear when the bedroom lights were turned off?
In the dark!

Why do teddy bears have furry ears?
So that they can hear!

What happens if a giant teddy bear
sits in front of you at the cinema?
Not much . . . but you don't get to
see much of the film!

Starbears

Rupert, Paddington, Superted and Winnie the Pooh are four of the biggest teddy bear superstars in the world. Here are a few pages put aside especially for them . . .

Where does Superted
get the special food
that makes him fly?
From the Supermarket!

Knock-knock!
Who's there?
Winnie-the
Winnie-the-Who?
No, Winnie-the-Pooh!

What's yellow, has two legs, but can't walk?
Rupert the Bear's trousers!

Why does Paddington wear bright red wellies?
To keep his feet dry!

What kind of marmalade does Paddington always take with him on a long car trip?
Traffic jam!

Paddington went to the Cinema to see his favourite film, but after a few minutes he got pins and needles in his paw and decided to stretch his little legs.

After a little walk up and down the

stairs, his paw felt much better, and so he went back to his seat . . . only to find a huge man sitting in his place.

"Excuse me," said Paddington "but that's my seat you're sitting in!"

"Prove it!" replied the nasty man.

"Well, you should find that I left my marmalade sandwich on it!"

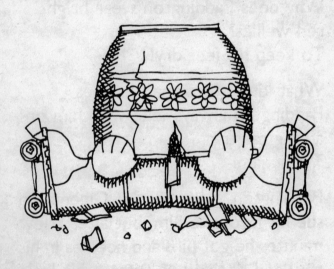

What happened to Paddington when he rollerskated into the china shop? He had a smashing time!

How did Winnie-the-Pooh get sticky fur?
By using a honey-comb!

Pooh eats peas with honey.
He's done it all his life.
They do taste rather funny,
But it keeps them on the knife!

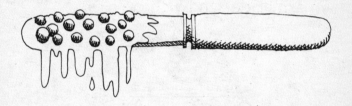

Rupert had a cold, but went to school because he had to do a spelling test. He was given his score, and was so excited that he ran back home immediately to tell his mother how he'd done. He ran inside and said, with a rather blocked up nose:

"Bubby, bubby . . . I've got the results of the spelling test!!"

"Well, tell me Rupert," Mum asked, "How did you do?"

"I got full barks!" replied Rupert, "Ted out of Ted!"

Why is it so difficult for Winnie-the-Pooh to get honey in Bristol?
Because there's only one "B" in Bristol!

How did Paddington manage to eat so much marmalade on Christmas day?
He got up early!

What happened to Superted when he got stuck trying to fly out of his house through the chimney?
He was the toast of the town!

Teacher: If the shop was selling 2 tins of peanut butter for £1, and I gave you 50p ... what would you get?
Paddington: A jar of marmalade!

Pooh Bear: I keep seeing jars of honey in my sleep!
Tigger: Have you seen a doctor?
Pooh Bear: No, only jars of honey!

What's this?

The Bearolympics

After lunch, and then after a little snooze, it's very important for teddy bears to keep fit by taking lots of exercise. Here are some jolly moments from the sporting world of the teddy bear.

What do you call a teddy bear that likes to ride a motorbike at 100 mph? A Bear-devil!

How did the teddy bear
beat the cheetah
in the 100 metre sprint?
He had a Ted-start!

What did the referees say when
Rupert and Paddington finished at
exactly the same time in the running
race?
They declared it a Ted-heat!

Why didn't the teddy manage to
break the round-the-world flying
speed record for a jet aircraft?
He went in a hot bear balloon!

Which sea did Rupert swim across to
break the world long-distance
swimming record?
The Ted-iterranean!

How do you start a teddy bear
running race?
Ready, Teddy, Go!

Where do teddy bears hope to hold
the next Olympics?
Bear-mingham!

61

How do teddy bears keep fit?
They do a lot of Bear-obics!

What's the difference between going
to support the teddy bear Olympics
and sunbathing?
In one, you're backing a bear, and in
the other you're bearing your back!

What do you do to a teddy bear that
smells?
Put a clothes peg on his nose!

What did the teddy bear call the book of his life-story?
His auto-bear-ography!

Why can't polar bears keep secrets?
Because they can't stop their teeth chattering in the cold weather!

What's the difference between a supermarket cashier and Winnie-the-Pooh?
One hates money, but the other one's mate is honey!

What did the French teddy bear call his pet dog?
Winnie-the-Poodle!

What do you call a horse with smelly feet?
Whinny . . . the Pooh!

What's the hardest thing facing a teddy bear on the flying-trapeze?
The floor!

What do you get if you cross a
teddy with a cow and a baby
goat?
A milky bear-kid!

What's the scariest teddy bear
horror movie?
Paws!

What happens when you cross a
teddy bear with a woodpecker?
You get a bear that speaks in morse
code!

What's a teddy bear
when he's a thief?
A bear-glur!

What do you call a bear from outer-
space?
E.T. . . . the Extra-Ted-estrial!

What do you get if you cross a teddy
bear with a toaster?
A bear that keeps popping out all
night!

What do you get if you cross a teddy with a monkey?
A swinging-bear!

When is a polar bear
not a polar bear?
When he's in
a grizzly mood!

Humph!

How do teddies send their letters?
By bear mail!

What do you call a teddy bear that
never breaks the rules?
A very paw-abiding citizen!

Where do bears dry their clothes?
In the bear-ing cupboard!

What do you get if
you cross a teddy bear
with a magic spell?
A-Bear-Cadabra!

Baby bear woke up one morning in a very curious mood. There seemed to be so many things he wanted to know about — but nobody ever told him anything about anything. So, he went downstairs and asked his daddy:

"Dad, why is the sky blue?"

"I've no idea, son" replied Daddy.

"Oh, well ... er ... why do birds sing?"

"I've no idea, son!" replied Daddy again.

"Never mind, but ... er ... why does the wind blow?"

"I've no idea, son!" replied Daddy ... yet again!

"You don't mind me asking all these questions do you, Dad?"

"Of course not, son. You'll never learn anything unless you ask!"

Why do teddy bears wear fur coats?
Because they'd look rather silly in
red, shiny macs!

How is a skunk different from a teddy
bear?
They use a different deodorant!

How does a teddy bear keep the fur
on his head tidy at night?
He uses a bear-net!

Where do polar bears go to dance?
A Snowball!

How do teddy bears
dress on a cold day?
Very quickly!

bear arm

bear
bottom

bear
leg

Big bear in the kitchen: Why is your
name Flannel?
Little bear in the kitchen: Because I
shrink from washing!

Why do you need three teddy bears
in the kitchen?
One to wash up, one to dry up and
one to pick up the pieces!

How do you make a teddy bear's
furry coat last?
You make his furry trousers first!

It is truly said that teddy bears brighten up a bedroom . . . they never turn out the light!

What do you get if you cross a teddy bear with a kangaroo?
A teddy bear jumper with pockets!

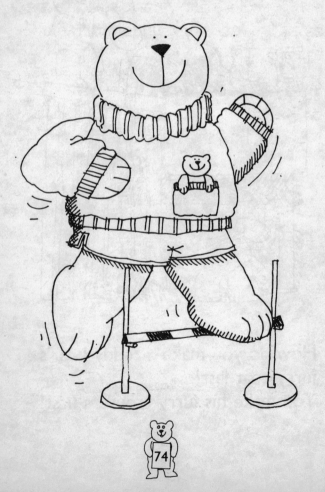

Bears Away!

All teddy bears deserve a break from time to time . . . so remember to take your teddy with you when you next go away somewhere (but don't put him in your nasty, dark suitcase because it gets very uncomfortable in there!).

What do teddy bears take with them on holiday?
Nothing but the bear-essentials!

How do teddy bears get to their holiday resorts?
By bear-o-plane!

Which company do they fly with?
British bear-ways!

Teddy: I'm going on holiday to the Alps, and I would like a new fur coat, please!
Shop assistant: Certainly Sir ... what fur?
Teddy: To keep me warm, of course!

How does a teddy bear take all his medicines before going away on holiday?
He has them inject-Ted!

What language did the twin teddy bears speak in Holland?
Double-Dutch!

Where do Australian teddy bears go scuba-diving?
The Great Bear-ier Reef!

Why do very tall teddy bears get better sun-tans than very short teddy bears?
They lie longer in the sun!

What did Captain Bear say to make
the ship go faster?
Full speed a-Ted!

Which teddy bear needs the biggest
sun-hat?
The one with the biggest head!

What kind of parties do
teddy bears throw during
their Summer holidays?
Bear-b-queues!

Knock, knock.
Who's there?
Soup!
Soup who?
Superted!

Pandamonium

Pandas are very adventurous bears. They love exploring and playing new games. Sometimes they get into a bit of a pickle . . .

What's black and white and very noisy?
A panda with a set of drums!

What's black and white but red all over?
A panda with sunburn!

What's black and white, got four legs and a trunk?
Two pandas on holiday!

What's black and white, and goes click-click!
A ball-point panda!

What's black and white and goes up and down?
A panda stuck in a lift!

What's black and white, has a mane, six legs and a tail?
A panda on a horse!

What's black and white and goes round and round . . . and round?
A panda stuck in a revolving door!

What's black and white and stands in the corner?
A naughty panda!

What's black and white, has eight
wheels and travels very fast?
A panda on roller-skates!

What's black and white on the inside
and green on the outside?
A panda disguised as a cabbage!

What's black and white and goes
through tunnels very quickly?
A panda on the underground!

What's black and white and yellow?
A scared panda!

What's black and white and bounces?
A rubber panda!

What's black, white and blue?
A sad panda!

What goes black-and-white, black-and-white and downwards?
A panda rolling down a hill!

What goes "Black-and-white-ha-ha"?
The panda that pushed him!

Jack: I dreamt last night that I needed
a licence to have a teddy bear!
Jill: Really? What kind of teddy bear
did you have . . . a big brown bear?
Jack: No!
Jill: A red bear?
Jack: No!
Jill: A pink bear?
Jack: No!
Jill: What kind, then?
Jack: A panda!
Jill: Why did you have a panda?
Jack: Because a black and white
licence was cheaper than a colour
one!

What's this?

A Koala bear climbing the far side of a tree!

Jack: I hear that the Police are looking for a bear with one eye called Nelson Teddy!
Jill: What's his other eye called?

What happened to the teddy bear who slept with his head under the pillow?
He woke up in the morning to find that the fairies had come, and taken all his teeth!

If a Panda called Ching-Chong went to Hong Kong to play Ping-Pong and have a Sing-Song ... what noise did his doorbell make?
Buzz!

Where do you find wild teddy bears?
It depends where you leave them!

If a brown teddy bear fell into the
Red Sea, how would it come out?
Wet!

What do you do with a blue teddy
bear?
You try to cheer him up!

Why do purple teddy bears eat less than brown teddy bears?
There are fewer of them!

Which side of a teddy bear is the furriest?
The outside!

Why do bears lose weight when there are no bees about?
Because if you take the "B" out of "bear", they become like "air".

Why is the letter "D" like a bear's tummy-button?
Because they're both in the middle of Teddy!

What do you look like when you take a bath?
A little bear!

If a teddy bear holds fifteen apples in one paw, and fourteen apples in the other, what does he have?
Mighty big paws!

Who was surprised to be the first
king of all the bears?
Ethel-Ted the Unready

What did one bear say to the other
bear when he got onto the front page
of the newspaper?
Golly, you're in the Ted-lines!

What's this?

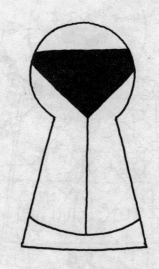

The view of Teddy's nose through a
keyhole!

What's black and white with red spots?
A panda with measles!

Father bear: Who's been sleeping in my bed?
Mother bear: Who's been sleeping in my bed?
Baby bear: Who's been zzzzzzzzzzzzz
.... zzzzzzzzzzzzzzzzzzzzzzz
THE END